T0078042

DANCING
WITH THE
MYSTERY

SAIGE

ARCHWAY
PUBLISHING

Archway Publishing books may be ordered
through booksellers or by contacting:

Archway Publishing
1663 Liberty Drive
Bloomington, IN 47403
www.archwaypublishing.com
844-669-3957

ISBN: 978-1-6657-5546-7 (sc)
ISBN: 978-1-6657-5547-4 (e)

Library of Congress Control Number: 2024900754

Print information available on the last page.

Archway Publishing rev. date: 02/05/2024

To: Love. In this lifetime and beyond.
To the brave hearts and courageous souls who
know there's more to life than what meets the eye.

Contents

al·che·my:
/ˈalkəmē/
a seemingly magical process of
transformation, creation, or combination

Dream Guidance

"GET BACK HERE." I woke from the sound of a voice in my dream. A loud masculine voice - familiar. Stern but not violent. More like the assertive, loving protector. Using his assertiveness to get the message across.

It shook me.

I recognized the voice to be that of Ku - the Hawai'ian God who I'd been in study of. The story of how he sacrificed his life to protect and feed his family — and the prolific Ulu tree that grew to sustain nourishment throughout a famine had made a mark on my spirit. I connected with him while visiting the Islands and thought him to be a powerful representation of the divine masculine.

When he came to me that night in Dreamtime, I knew what he wanted...

It was another cold, wet morning in the Olympic Peninsula. I was lying half-awake on the loft of my seaside A-frame home where my husband, Jonah, and I had spent hours arranging and rearranging, designing furniture and creating a space that felt like a temple.

The call to the Islands had first begun when I was ripe and pregnant with my first-born daughter. I'd visited Kaua'i and between the salty ocean on my skin, swimming with turtles and feeling the energy of the lands — my heart broke when it was time to return to the mainland. The Islands had felt like home in a way I'd never known... my tears upon driving to the airport felt like they were informing me of my true desire and acknowledging that it would take a journey to get back to where my heart wanted to be.

It had been years since then — we had made a few visits back to the Islands and many signs and synchronicities continued to whisper an invitation. The courage to answer the call didn't come easily though... there were many reasons to stay planted where we were. So little evidence and what felt like no safety net to uproot the family and go somewhere without community.

Oh, but that quiet little whisper. She was persistent. The bumper stickers of hibiscus flowers, the half coconut shell washing up on the winter beach one day, the feeling in my heart that remained no matter how hard I tried to quiet her voice and pretend to be home where I was.

After the dream — it was clear.

Intuition

The primal part of us that already knows the answers to the questions we seek. The softest, yet most persistent voice always guiding us in the direction that's most true to our soul.

Intuition is like the wise grandmother inside of us. She knows the solution but loves us enough to not take away our freewill and discovery process. She knows that the journey of twists and turns to uncover our truth is a vital part of our growth. So quietly she sits, hands folded, awaiting our arrival, yet not rushing us through the process.

Dream Journal

Dec 31

"Today is the last day of the year. My dreams last night were clear, vivid, and powerful.

I was a young woman, a maiden who fell in love with the most handsome, tall, kind man. It felt challenging because I was in partnership - deeply domestic and committed to someone else. He also had a lover. A young, flashy, and beautiful woman. There were moments of sadness and desire - though mostly a deep knowing that even though it would require strength - being with the true love was the right thing to do. One evening, after a day together (we worked together?) his lady came to pick him up. I ran out of the room emotional - in tears. He came after me and we melted into our love and kissed - we decided to be together and face the challenges that would come with that decision. It felt like a true homecoming and a deep sigh of relief.

To me, this morning I feel like it signifies our move to Hawai'i.

The true love that requires leaving behind the old, the comfortable and familiar. The heart always knows what will nourish it."

The Call

The call of the Islands remained. Through songs, signs, a deep knowing in my heart.

In many ways it would have been easier to stay on the mainland. Our home was anchored, the community was lovely, nothing was wrong per se. Except for a quiet knowing that it was no longer home...

If I hadn't gone back to visit the Islands ever again, I could have tried to push down the desire and stayed complacent.

It was when we returned for a third time that it was impossible to deny. The call was so strong and as usual it spoke through the body.

I didn't get on our return flight home — I couldn't. The kids and I stayed with a friend as Jonah went back to find renters for our home, quit his job and return to our new life.

We were taking a leap of faith and jumping headfirst into the mystery. I was signaling to myself and the unseen forces that it was time for my career to fully flourish because there was no plan b. For this family, there was no trust fund or safety net other than God.

When we finally answered the call to the Islands — I created a public listing asking to steward land as we weren't fully ready to sell our home and commit to life full time on the Aina.

Within a few hours, we had a response with an invitation to manage a ten-acre avocado farm on the West side of the Island — in the exact location my heart felt most pulled. We agreed, sight unseen — and weeks later moved our family of four into to a tiny rustic studio on one of the most gorgeous plots of land overlooking the sea. It was a humbling shift after so much re-modeling and putting finishing touches on our Temple home, but the guidance was there and as usual, we were following it.

I would meditate nightly. I'd hear the voice of the divine that I came to trust so well — that intuitive voice would tell me that this is where we were being stationed to learn to be like the lotus in the mud. While the view was gorgeous, and the fruit trees abundant — there was a lot of mess from the old coffee mill operation on the land — years of old, dense energy to clean up and part of our divine assignment for that time was to be there and purify the lands. I would hear that everything we poured into there would transfer over with us, and to stay the course even when things got challenging with the politics of managing people.

That land not only became our first Island home, but also became my school, my church, the most humbling training grounds to remember who I was and what I incarnated to this Earth to do.

As the world shut down for the pandemic — there was nowhere to go but deeper into connection with the Earth. It was there that I began to vision life in Village community. I started to be able to not just connect to the land in a spiritual sense, but to truly hear the voices of the trees and the secret spirits and guardians of the Earth. It was there that I learned how to be in reciprocal relationship and direct conversation with the land — to work with the energies present to build not only what we desired but what the land willed as well.

Our time at the farm was transformational. It was often challenging for many reasons, though every time I wanted to leave, the voice would guide us back to feeling confident to stay the course. That we were there on purpose, on a mission.

A Catalyst for Awakening

During my first pregnancy I began to wake up to the many quiet ways the wild in me had been tamed. It was my anxiety that led me to first open the door to peek inside the inner paradigms that had been unconsciously running my life. I knew that becoming a mother would require a certain kind of spiritual resilience and calm - one I knew existed but felt foreign and out of reach. I had spent years repressing and fearing the anxiety that was bubbling up - it had gotten to a point where it was hard to track when and where the energy would arise. It became a fear of the fear - dread that my body would forsake me while driving, or randomly in a store or conversation with someone. I felt like my own body was betraying me - I didn't yet understand that she was trying to get my attention to open me up to the most important conversation of my life.

Anxiety was my catalyst. My gateway into remembering my truth and wholeness. Had I shamed, pushed it down, continued to run or popped a pill the way society prescribes - I'm sure that I would be still battling that demon to this day.

Instead, I went in towards the suffering. There was a deep, primal call within me to address this messenger before giving birth to new life.

I'd been learning about the power of the subconscious mind through my hypno-birthing course and decided to book myself a real hypnotherapy session to address the symptoms for the last time.

My practitioner was a lovely, gentle mother who felt easy to trust and feel safe with. Once I was in trance, she guided me to connect with my subconscious mind by visualizing it as a shape. It appeared to me as a giant floating bird. An animal that's come to me many times since then.

She guided me to gently inquire with this part of me on why I had been going into fight or flight so frequently, what was the purpose?

I heard my confident response leaving my lips before my mind could keep up with the fact that it was me speaking. "To protect you." were the words that slipped out.

To protect me? That was it? That was the reason my brain would signal to my body that I was dying at random moments on any occasion? Thank you, but no thank you.

In this gentle trance state, I was guided to ask my subconscious gently but confidently to kindly find another way to protect me.

It felt so simple and obvious.

I left the office knowing something had just changed majorly in my life. Like I had just remembered something important that I could not believe I'd forgotten... and I never had a panic attack again.

It was that pregnancy that finally re-awakened me to my psychic powers I had long forgotten.

At first a gentle stirring and then a louder, fiercer remembrance of my true self, my ability to directly hear my ancestors, the divine assignment that had been placed on me in this lifetime to bring forth creation from my womb.

I started to remember my body's natural ability to carry and birth life without intervention - a truth I had to peel back layers and layers of unconscious conditioned fear to reclaim.

In pregnancy, I became a gentle warrior. At first subscribing to the outer guidance, opinions, and noise from people all around me, and eventually tuning it out and listening in more and more to my own wisdom and the voice of my first growing baby.

How strange, I thought — that I had never once attended a birth and witnessed a new human life emerging. That the most naturally occurring phenomena in existence was hidden away and made taboo, cloaked in a film of fear and distortion.

I knew in my bones that my body was designed to birth my baby safely without medical intervention — and after learning what I did about the subconscious mind, I devoted myself to re-coding that unconscious part of me to know it too.

I did energy work to clear medical trauma and memories from childhood, and hypnosis to re-program my mind to know that birth was safe and that mine would be the perfect experience for me and my child. Nightly, Jonah and I would listen to audio recordings about how my body would blossom and open like a flower when it was time for my Tula to arrive Earthside.

When she finally did arrive, it was a long labor, almost 3 days long to be exact. It was not the simple blissful 5-hour labor I was hoping for, but it was the exact ego-death, warrior training, soul awakening, motherhood initiation that I needed.

Birth

Birth. I believe part of the reason I choose to incarnate as a woman is so that I can forget and remember again the raw beauty of birth. The portal between time and space realities. The most intimate dance with the mystery of all.

Tula

I could write books about Tula. My first born. My fiery hearted, passionate, courageous force to be reckoned with of a daughter. She came into this world with a bang. In many ways she has been my awakener. I felt her circling me closely before becoming pregnant - I missed her before I met her and answered her call to come Earthside during a passionate and spontaneous moment of love making with Jonah.

I was twenty-six years old and so ready to be a mother but not prepared in the least for the reality of it. Maybe nothing can prepare you for that initiation of a lifetime. I knew it would be a challenge but then my fiery, high needs, sensitive soul of a child was born into my arms and, damn. The birth itself was a foreshadowing to the experience of mothering. Three long days and nights of laboring until finally, with the rise of the full moon - my Scorpio daughter arrived into this world.

She was my yoga ball baby. She needed constant movement and soothing to be content. She seemed to cry louder than the other babies, only sleep for twenty minutes at a time and challenge me in ways I could not have even fathomed. In my brief years of childcare for other families - I had never met a baby with this much force. It was as though she was enraged at being born into an infant body and was ready to express in ways her vessel wouldn't yet allow.

I remember looking around at other "normal" babies wondering what I was doing wrong - or why I had been graced with this baby that felt impossible at times. I felt guilty for resenting her nature that exhausted me to the bone. I came to learn that Tula, like me, seemed to have come to this planet with a specific mission. Her first medicinal offering to me would be reminding me of my own energetic sensitivities. It was through observing her keen awareness to environment and sensations and almost neurotic psychic awareness that I could see my own. Her freedom to express and feel rage and pain like I've never seen in anyone, was matched with the brightest joy and ecstasy on the other side of the spectrum - she reminded me of how to feel it all and repress nothing.

As years went by, she became more and more comfortable in her human body. Learning to work with the flowing energies and occupy her senses with new things to explore and learn. Last week after a day of overwhelm and high emotions she went to the spices, opened them, and began to calm her own nervous system.

Now, at age eight Tula is one of the most emotionally intelligent, attuned, and compassionate beings I know.

She's still got the fierce unfuckable-with spirit that pushes my patience and inspires me in equal parts. She's a powerhouse, a magician, a light beam, and a gift to this world. Watching her grow into herself is one of my life's greatest honors.

The Mother

The Mother is the life giver - the portal to creation - yet somehow, somewhere, culture lost the priority of nourishing the mother - honoring her wise and mature leadership and codes of unconditional love - making sure the village was centered around pouring back into her so she could pour into the ones she was raising - the future creators of reality.

Somehow, we began to lust after the hyper masculine templates of success and even "feminism" took on this costume of empowerment through external success and hyper productivity.

The woman moving through the initiation into motherhood was no longer made to feel as though she was accessing the honor of life's greatest rite of passage through birthing and nurturing life - but that rather her worth was now reduced.

As society pushed her existence to the side, not so subtly conveyed that her body was now less beautiful, shamed her for exposing her beautiful breasts they once obsessed over as she publicly fed her baby - all while offering a pull-your-bootstraps-up side eye.

I remember feeling the stress as a young mother when my children would throw a tantrum publicly. As though somehow, I could have been doing a better job to manage their emotions.

No.

The world could have been doing a better job to allow space for the range of human expression to exist and for the mother to be held as she was expected to hold her young.

Ayahuasca

I first sat ceremony with Ayahuasca in a small town in Peru. I was traveling with my friend at the time who I'd later fall in love with and have some important karmic lessons to learn. I was young, in my twenties living the urban life in New York and I didn't know much about Ayahuasca's medicines — she was a mystery to me. My decision to hop in a dusty cab and drive hours into the middle of the rural Amazonian jungle to a town called Infierno to seek out a renowned indigenous shaman was based less on holistic healing and more so on spontaneity and adventure. Or so I thought.

The power and the potency of my experience in this middle of nowhere river ceremony would re-direct my life path in such rapid and unrelenting way. When I arrived home to New York, it was so clear it was no longer my home — that this urban lifestyle was over. I left the city and never went back. The journey had re-opened my eyes to my connection with the Earth and I knew in my heart I was meant to prioritize that connection and live somewhere I could breathe freely and immerse myself in nature.

The journey was so powerful, I let it slow steep and integrate for a decade. She didn't beckon me to sit with her again until exactly ten years later when we were living on the Island.

I heard her call and shortly after received an invitation to sit ceremony on a beautiful piece of land across the Island.

At the time — I was deeply immersed in life on the farm and anchoring the first template for re-villaging. I was getting downloads and insights about how life could be living in community — not in the hippie commune way, but in a truly enlightened society.

By then, we had moved our family into the main house on the land and a former client turned soul sister Amara had come to live next to us in our old ohana. She became an auntie to my children and daily we were getting to experience life in these higher states of consciousness, and soulful communion. We'd do breathwork together, dance, create beauty and channel guidance about the land.

We decided to go together to the ceremony.

The Ceremony

When we first arrived to the land - the familiar judgmental mind surfaced the way it can when one is in new and unfamiliar territory. In my heart, I was keeping the exit door open - there were no absolutes here and if at any moment this mysterious invitation didn't feel resonant, I had no objections to leaving. It felt challenging to separate the nerves from excitement - I found myself scanning the room and the people there trying to find confirmation or make sense of my place here. Amara and I left to get our belongings from the car and get settled in. Moving forward despite the nerves, witnessing ourselves making continuous motions to be there despite all the chatter of the mind.

Before we walked back to the pagoda - I felt the urge to channel into the land. We dropped our pace and found a place on a quiet hillside where we were out of sight from the gathering.

Amara, being the Earth queen that she is, recognized a ceremony when she heard one and dropped immediately down to the ground - I remained standing my ground, barefoot.

I closed my eyes and dropped into that familiar place that I had been to so many hundreds of times.

I felt the shift of energies, my body began to buzz, and I heard the gentle and calm voice of spirit move through me once again.

"This is about the land. Try to refrain from judging other people or the structures, - be where you are and feel into the conversation this land invited you to have with her. This is a special place with things to teach you. You are safe here; you are held, and you can trust yourself that you are exactly where you are meant to be."

I sensed the energy of another presence and blinked open my eyes to see walking up the hill was a man with blonde hair and this angelic face - serene and ethereal yet strong and grounded. I felt both the abruptness of his interruption but also as though I had been expecting his arrival somehow.

As he got closer, he smiled and asked us our names.

I introduced us both and responded, asking if he was who I spoke with on the phone.

His presence matched the voice, and I recognized him somehow. He affirmed and welcomed us. We had some light conversation before continuing in separate directions.

Where the energy once had felt unsettled, it now felt smooth. The channeled message made it clear at least to me that this was where we were meant to be. I looked around and noticed the most beautiful, thriving Ulu trees were lining the property - like divine masculine protectors at the threshold.

Amara seemed to have felt relaxed by the transmission as well as we both felt ready to make our way back into the pagoda to wait for the night to draw closer and the ceremony to begin.

We settled into the room, trying to find a comfortable space to create a nest for the evening. The room was packed and crowded; all pillows were already spoken for. We located a corner in the very back of the room that had the last few feet of space open. We headed over and began laying our pillows.

As I was preparing to spread my bed out, Amara nudged me to turn around and save space for the person who came in behind me.

It was the same man with the angelic face. He had entered the room last and was attempting to take a seat in the last inches of space available in the room - that happened to be at my feet.

I remembered feeling slightly annoyed at his presence because it meant surrendering the comfortable nest I was attempting to create for myself with my bed. I rolled up my mat to create space for the kind stranger - sat down, closed my eyes and began to meditate.

The ceremony began. In walked the Maestro accompanied by his beautiful, otherworldly assistant. The candles were lit, the sage was burned and finally, the tea was served. One-by-one we made our way up to the front to be offered our portion and blessed before returning back to our seats to experience our individual journey.

My experience can be described in multiple phases:

The meditation, the healing, the horror, the surrender and finally (finally) the purge.

I sat in silent contemplation, feeling the effects soon after - at first in a slow, delicious unfurling. There began the kaleidoscope of my life - my loves, the gratitude I held for each being I knew. I was in the meditation phase of my journey and so far, it was just as I remembered it - a mystical and effervescent experience of oneness, gratitude and forgiveness.

The music began. It was hauntingly beautiful and seemed to float right into the visions I was having and carry me deeper into my own journey, I began to slowly lose interest in the beings around me and suddenly all at once - the medicine amplified.

It felt like it was more than I could bear. I was taken from this soft and mystical planet into this intense experience that was overtaking my body. I knew suddenly that I wasn't able to stay contained in this room alongside all these other energies. I could hear the voice of Mother Earth beckoning me to leave and step outside. She had the energy of a fierce and loving Mother who was no longer fooling around. I didn't know what she wanted to say to me, but I knew I had no choice but to answer her call.

I left the room and walked outside to see the moon sparkling over the luminescent grass which seemed to now have this visible glimmering life of its own. I observed the momentary bliss I was able to experience despite the feeling of overwhelming physical sensations and visuals. I felt sick to my stomach and found a place to drop down to the Earth and bury my face in the soil.

I laid there in misery. Sick, surrendered and knowing outside under the moon with only myself and the Earth as my guides - was exactly where I was meant to be.

At some point I heard a gentle voice approach me and recognized it as the man with the angelic face. He asked me if I needed anything to which I responded that I simply needed to be left alone with the Earth. He understood and offered a blanket, which I declined.

As he was walking away, I heard my own voice follow his asking - "hey- do you know if there's any way to make this nausea go away?"

He approached once more and softly replied - slightly stuttering over his own words. "There aren't really human words for this type of experience. Just follow your heart. Try to be the witness."

Throughout the night he would continue to tend to me, occasionally, quietly. Keeping a distance yet a steady presence that reminded me I wasn't entirely alone on this journey. He felt like an energetic doula to my personal rebirth, and I was grateful for his distant presence.

I laid hunched over in the grass for what felt like years.

I knew this journey was intended to be about me and the land - but I didn't anticipate being in such a direct conversation. I laid there in misery, wishing I could just vomit and be done with the whole experience. I wanted out.

I heard the voice of the Mother asking me to surrender. "I am!" I winced. "More." She replied.

How could I possibly surrender more? Here I am, a woman in her thirties, lying face down in the soil, begging the grass for relief, literally saying I will do anything - and this isn't surrendered enough?

She explained to me that I was only surrendering because I wanted to feel relief. I was doing it for myself.

She had a point.

I began to ask her how I could surrender even more. I told her I would do anything to have this discomfort taken away from me. I told her I was here; I could feel her frustration with me, and I was ready to listen in to what she had been asking of me.

This voice of the divine mother spirit began to explain to me that life was full of challenges and learning to be with the discomfort was far more noble than always looking for the easy way out. She told me relief wouldn't come until I could surrender into the acceptance of the present. She mentioned how I had been moving around the world almost like an entitled teenager, resenting my incarnation onto this planet, thinking it was lighter and brighter out there in the beyond.

She reminded me of how much I love it here. What an honor it is to be able to come to Earth - the sensate pleasures, the beauty, the natural world that provides us anything we could ever need. She reminded me of how excited I was to come to this planet and asked me to promise that all my future endeavors be in direct honor of her.

I cried.

She was right. This planet didn't always feel the most comfortable for as sensitive of a being as myself. There had been times when I wanted out. I had been resenting the confusion of modern society and somehow placing blame onto her as though that was her fault.

I could see so clearly now that it wasn't.

That she, Earth, this sentient entity was far different than the overlay of society erected upon her. I devoted myself to her service, and this time I meant it.

I purged. The most challenging part of my journey was over and now I could go rest.

Back inside I returned to my little corner and curled into a ball.

I could feel Amara oscillating between tears and ecstasy - and felt glad to be back in her proximity with my awareness returning slowly. Ceremony was coming to a close and all I wanted to do was sleep.

I started to drift off to sleep as the man with the angelic face approached to tell us goodbye. We exchanged a few kind words before he began packing up his things while singing a gentle song under his breath.

It was a song that went into my bones. I felt like I had heard it a million times before and also like it was the first time it was ever sung.

_____

The next morning, I returned to the other side of the Island and back to my life. I knew that ceremony had been a major one and that the tectonic plates of my life were already shifting... but I didn't anticipate how much.

That night, I went to take the garbage out and hit my hand on the wood panel above the cabinet — I looked down to see my wedding ring had broken.

Soft Whispers

When I think back to my early twenties and how lost I sometimes felt — I wish I could go back and hug myself and tell her how she was exactly where she was meant to be. All the confusion, the wrong turns, the fucking up — the partying, dropping out of college. It was all perfect.

I realize now I was simply seeking then, what I have tools to practice now. An altered state of consciousness that would make my role on this Earthly plane make more sense.

A place to feel connected instead of separate. A return to a more familiar dimension outside of the density of the illusion.

The difference is that in my twenties I didn't have tools to access the Truth in the way I do now. I looked for it outside of me - in others. I blamed others for my pain instead of feeling into the triggers they showed me. I drank myself into oblivion. I broke heart after heart as a way to feel powerful and avoid the rawness of true intimacy.

The world felt too much for me - too beautiful, too tragic - too loud and violent. No one had ever trained me in depth to trust my inner knowing's and the soft whispers of the voice of spirit.

Remembrance

The man with the angelic face didn't go away.

Weeks later I would rise in the night – jolted awake from a dream. It was him again.

Then, it happened again. And then again. I would wake up suddenly, drenched in my own tears, shaking from a feeling of longing. Who was this man and why was I having such a strong reaction to him?

I tried to bury the feelings — they felt inconvenient and completely dis-proportional. Since he wasn't in my everyday life, I figured he was serving as some kind of metaphor.

Over the months, his energy continued to visit me and I started to get curious about our connection.

I would be driving with my kids in the middle of the day, suddenly feel his presence unexpectedly and would burst into tears.

One day, the first memory came.

It was in a vision of a past life — we were young lovers, 19 or 20 or so... We met while he was on a voyage by boat. He had stopped in my port town; we fell in love, and I decided to go with him and his crew on their travels. On the boat we began to plan our life. The babies we'd have, the home we'd build.

When he drowned a couple of months later, I was distraught. I had given up everything I knew to be with this man. He was the love of my life, and we had a future... and now he was gone.

When I saw into that life, the feelings I was having in the present made more sense. It was almost like the grief of this young woman was alive in me now, like my subconscious couldn't separate this man from being my dead fiancé — even though that's not who he was in the lifetime.

Why would he come back though?

When weeks later he sent a message with an invitation to return to another ceremony, I knew I had to go and resolve whatever this energy was.

The Second Ceremony

On the morning of the second ceremony a rainbow showed herself in the direction of the drive. As nervous as I was to go, I felt the confirmation of my journey being supported in the unseen realms and knew it was something that had to be done.

As I made my way across the Island – every fear threshold was brought to the surface. "Why am I doing this? What's the point? I should go back home."

I scanned my body again and felt the importance of the quest beyond what my mind could comprehend.

I weighed the risks. "What's the worst that could happen? I look crazy. My motives are misunderstood. His wife hates me. I sabotage a potential friendship…"

It was all worth it.

I had to tell this man what I was experiencing. I had never known this feeling before and didn't expect him to have the answer, but I knew I needed to free my heart of the pressure from this mysterious connection that was draining my life force. I figured if I couldn't close this feeling up on my own, maybe looking into his eyes would provide some kind of answer or key to why this was happening and how to complete it.

I kept driving.

I told myself I'd allow for the space to unfold organically for me to mention what I'd been feeling. He was married, and so was I — and I wanted to make sure to be in integrity with my sharing. To honor the energy that was present without creating any drama or distortion. I didn't exactly know what words I would speak but I was sure of my intentions: to speak truth and close up any old karma that was keeping me in this holding pattern of emotion. I wanted truth and freedom — for every party involved.

When I arrived that evening to the same pagoda, I found my place and settled in. When I met the facilitator of the night, I felt an immediate no and decided that evening to not drink the medicine, but to sit in space regardless. The hours that followed were almost as psychedelic as being on the medicine — I could feel the energy in the room pulse as everyone around me began to have their process.

I sat in stillness for hours, through my boredom, through my body discomfort, through my emotions and through my desire to leave. When the music finally came on in the end — I danced for hours in the dark.

After what felt like days, the ceremony finally came to a close.

Even though I didn't drink the tea, I'd had a huge cathartic journey just being in the space quantum entangled with the energies around me.

It was time to close out with gratitude and open the space for community sharing of words and music.

After a few songs — I felt someone else make their way to the center of the room and softly began to strum a guitar in the pitch dark. Within seconds - the grief was back. Consuming my body, I began to weep before recognizing the voice of the man with the angelic face.

He was singing a song of devotion to his wife and children – it was beautiful and pure, and his voice was so, so familiar.

I tried to silence my tears as they poured down my face. The emotion – again overtook me as though it was sourced from this otherworldly eternal place – somehow, I managed to keep an inaudible sound level as I felt the disproportionate heartbreak over this complete stranger.

If this really had been my lost love in a past life – why had he come back in this one? Why now? Was he feeling any kind of psychic connection too or was this only happening to me? I felt confused and exhausted and just wanted to go home.

Finally - it was all over and time for a late meal and connecting as a group.

Before anyone could speak to me, I slipped through the cabana door and ran through the pouring rain to my car.

This would be my bed for the evening. I threw myself down and wept harder than I could ever remember crying. For hours, I cried through the night. Defeated, exhausted, and confused.

I woke up before the rising sun and began to make my way back home before anyone else got up. I was ready to leave this land and never return.

My sadness had turned into anger.

I had journeyed all the way across the Island to face what felt like my divine assignment. I had to deliver this message but there hadn't been an opening so here it was, still bottled up inside.

I screamed.

When I made it home, I realized that I still needed to express myself even if no one else would ever hear it. I didn't expect others to understand what was happening – I didn't understand it myself. I pulled out my phone and began to record an audio of my experience with this other soul. I spoke it as though I was speaking directly to him: pouring my heart out yet staying with the simple facts. I didn't mention details about a romantic past life connection, just the profound familiarity I felt and how the disproportionate emotion was impacting my life.

For five minutes straight – I spoke the sincerest truth about how I'd never experienced anything like this before. How more than being curious if he felt anything similar, I wanted closure and to resolve these feelings of grief. I spoke with such authentic love, respect, and clarity and when I was done, I looked down at my phone to see a message had been received from him at the exact moment I finished.

He was checking in to make sure I was ok.

I pressed send on my recording.

It was impulsive but I also knew it had to be done – the synchronistic timing was there again, and the connection was something beyond me and any egoic desires.

I knew in that moment – regardless of how it was received, I was free.

Hours passed and finally a response:

"Thank you for sharing that. I can't say that I had any similar feelings or memories. I'm glad you were able to get some closure and am wishing you all the best."

That was it. Crystal clear – it had been an illusion after all. And if not, it was over either way. He didn't have the same feeling of familiarity or connection.

I felt the wave of relief wash over me and knew that the spontaneous waves of grief were over. I realized in that moment that I hadn't ever needed his validation – I had just needed to free myself and speak the truth. If I had the courage to speak that despite how it was received, I could now say anything, to anyone.

I paused before responding.

"Beautiful. There was no expectation of mutual recognition or experience. This was simply my unique soul curriculum as I initiate into a deeper understanding of our multidimensional nature. Mahalo for receiving with grace. All the best to you as well."

Only partly a lie. There was a subtle knife in the heart that he hadn't recognized my spirit when his had been so loud to me.

I had never believed in unrequited love. Even though it appeared as though it was over, I somehow knew in every cell of my body that nothing could dilute the purity of the connection I felt – even this dismissal.

The grief stopped. I moved on with my life. And then months later, he returned.

Seeking

If you're a seeker and you tend to seek - there's a good chance you'll never arrive fully at the thing you're seeking. Once one thing has been discovered - there's a new level of consciousness to explore. The mystery continues to unfold and spiral out to infinity. We are infinite beings - each containing multitudes. Sensitive souls are of another world - we volunteer to come back and raise consciousness but the density of the world in front of us may never fully make sense to us because in our hearts we remember another way.

In the Garden

When I was pregnant with my son Lux, all I wanted to do was garden. It was as if the spirit of the Earth herself was inside my womb, guiding me to connect to the plants and be directly on the soil. I would spend weekdays at the nursery with Tula, learning about which herbs and allies spoke directly to my soul. Bringing home plants by the dozen and spending the evenings reading books I checked out from the library on gardening. At the time - Jonah was providing for us and working for a very moderate wage and there was not a lot of extra. I spent whatever there was though on flowers, trees, and herbs - and felt all the richer for it.

It's funny how our seasons of life are so romantic as we reflect back upon them. At the time - I'm sure I felt swollen, emotional, uncertain about the transitions to becoming a mother of two - but when I look back now, I only remember the bliss of an easier and more confident pregnancy and my deepening connection to the Earth.

Lux

Lux is an angel on this Earth as far as I'm concerned. His frequency radiates this pure energy of the divine masculine. At age three he recalls his dreams with precision and detail. We can drive together in the car for an hour with neither of us saying a word but understanding each other completely. When he first began to speak it was mostly about flowers.

While pregnant with him I channeled that his name would mean "light." A few days later a friend gifted me a vintage baby name book. I was amused and even scoffed at it, recalling how Tula's name had been channeled direct from the source without the support of any media. She had told me her name and I anticipated this baby doing the same. I decided to look through the book anyway and came across the name "Lux" which sounded beautiful and mysterious to me. I wrote it down and went to look up the meaning and read "light." It was clear.

When he was born, I was in shock to see his radiant, porcelain skin - and that he had inherited none of my dark middle Eastern features I felt so proud of. He also had this white birthmark like a lightning bolt on the left side of his hair. "Light" I thought. "It really is you."

I went through waves of emotion processing his coloring in the weeks to follow - feeling some kind of guilt for being responsible for bringing another white man to the planet. I felt into the different experiences my children may have been born different genders with different color skin.

I hope by the time my children are old enough to really individuate and develop this sense of identity it has little to do with the exterior of their vessels and everything to do with how connected they feel to their spirits.

Sometimes when I look at Lux I want to burst into tears or laughter. It's almost too much. His energy feels like home to me, he's a calm, wise, playful teacher who has enriched my life in the most brilliant of ways.

When we lived like Fairies

In the months after returning from the ceremony, everything began to fall apart. Our time on the land we'd been managing was coming to a close. We made some offers on nearby farms, and nothing seemed to be working out. Much like after my first experience with the medicine in Peru — it seemed that everything that was no longer true in my life was commanding to be excavated.

In the stillness of meditation, I heard the voice again. "You must be willing to give it all up. All of it." I saw a vision of a graduation cap and gown and knew the lessons we needed to learn on the farm were complete. It was time to move on.

Doors continued to close as we sought our next home, and even temporary rentals were suddenly nonexistent. We considered liquidating and returning to the mainland – before hearing the call of the Earth one day to "come closer."

We decided to camp until the pathway forward felt clear. We stationed our family on a plot of land on a community member's acreage. We built a makeshift "house" out of wood platforms, a cover, and tents. We were living directly on the Earth now - no running water, no electricity - just us and the land.

One of my Kumus (teachers) at the time was an indigenous elder High Priestess. When I told her about our experience, she just laughed and laughed. She wasn't concerned. She reminded me that the modern-day initiations look different. She told me stories of her elders guiding her through specific trainings that had her camping for two years — if she wanted to eat; she hunted her own food. No grocery stores or modern conveniences. She told me other stories of being taken to the top of a mountain in the middle of the night and left alone to confront her deepest fears.

In her time and lineage there were specific trainings designed to cultivate inner strength and resilience. To become worthy of carrying the title of Kahuna, one must have devoted their life to training their intuitive gifts and demonstrated capacity to responsibly lead. This requires being humbled to your knees.

Being a Kahuna wasn't something you chose so much as the Heavens chose it for you before birth and you chose to train and rise into the calling or not.

For the modern-day mystic, the path is similar yet looks a little different. Since we don't necessarily come from cultures where the preservation of these trainings are intact, the young mystics are not often recognized by community and have to discover their gifts and train through life and seek out our own teachers.

The guardians and guides in the unseen will make sure we do not pass "go" until we follow the divine instructions laid out for us. There's still a training taking place, it's just being initiated by these unseen spirits who are dropping little hints and clues for where we go next. In my case, this means being taken to specific land sites to support the clearing of entities and activating of fresh energies. Sometimes supporting souls stuck in lower dimensions cross into higher ones.

Many souls who sign up to support the rise in consciousness will need to first study and train and go through a series of initiations so that they can steward their legacies in a way that is truly supportive to where humanity is heading.

So, when life didn't open doors for a short-term rental, we understood it was Earth calling us closer. We put all the kids' belongings in storage and told them we intended to live like fairies. My ego struggled with the idea - even though my heart was excited for the adventure of living in this kind of simplicity - "what will people think?" haunted the background noise of my mind.

How do you explain to mainstream society - "oh I'm good - I'm actually just going through an initiation right now?" It's like speaking another language. You're met with concerned looks, projections of judgements, cocked heads of doubt every time.

Living life in accordance with the divine assignment means becoming very resilient - you have to cultivate a thick skin and inner unshakeable confidence that can withstand the perceptions of others. Tula was in the local Waldorf school at the time and when her teacher discovered our turn of fate - she wrote to me lovingly expressing that she hoped everything would soon "fall into place" for our family.

I reminded her that it already had.

This is what culture does. Pities others that are going through trying times as if life is about some utopian destination instead of the amount of grace we bring through the journey. Those who know that life is always falling apart to come back together, to fall apart again; know that the inner gold comes from the greatest challenges. We don't whimper at the de-tours. We may grieve, cry, kick, howl, scream while it's happening - but we do not avoid or suppress a thing.

It occurred to me while living outside that the majority of people are orchestrating their lives in ways that will look good to others even if it means paying the price of feeling good on the inside. We tell children to go to school, build the career, create the world's vision of "success" - but at what cost?

When we returned to living outside, we lived like fairies. We were aware of our footprint, where our water came from and how much garbage we created. We consumed little material objects and made great use of what we had. We ate food from the land and spent evenings looking at the stars. We re-aligned our nervous systems to be in harmony with the circadian rhythms of the natural world. There was no Netflix, no desire to stay up too late. There wasn't even a house to spend all day cleaning. It was just us and the Earth and our test of all time to be present with simplicity and returning home to our Truth.

Dream Journal

Feb 2022

"I'm so glad to be staying on the Island. This feels like home to my soul. I'd rather be on this land fully here while camping on the Earth than in the creature comforts on the mainland. This has been an adventure - a full on surrender and deep listening. An answer to a calling.

Leading up to this moment felt like one of the most intense dark nights - fear, terror, pain, frustration, confusion. It all melted away once we decided to stay at all costs."

Surrender

"I want what my God Self wants" became my mantra that year while in the throes of surrender to the deepest, most humbling portal of transformation. Everything I had built was dismantled. I tried to cling on to familiarity, but soul had another plan. To surrender to the mystery.

Many of us say we want liberation but are we willing to let go of what we already know? We want to hold on to the guardrails of life, save appearances, play it safe in the familiar. That's not where freedom lives though. Freedom lives in the spaces where we meet our own edges, challenge former beliefs about what's possible to create, follow the mysterious breadcrumbs to a whole new existence of reality.

When doors won't open no matter how hard we try, sometimes it's because we're simply knocking on the wrong door. Sometimes we're simply being called to a new door – the one that makes our heart rush thinking about it. That one that scares us completely but also tastes like freedom. That one that feels like the most uncertain mystery but also somehow like home.

A Vision

I saw a Queen of the moon. Stoic, calm, independent, mysterious - other worldly. Quiet and noble, away from the mess of the loud third dimension. She was huge, long hair, and wanted to show me a vision on Earth. She showed me myself on the other side of the Island. Long hair, strong, holding a baby. The message was given to "listen." - I cried. I received guidance to let go of relationships that have unclean energy or keep me smaller or less authentic. To move in towards those that compliment my royalty - expand my visions and call me forward toward my mission. She told me to be in the company of living masters. To have many relationships but to walk intimately alongside only very few. To have lengthy periods of quiet on the Earth in conversation with my soul and Gaia. To love everything yet be attached to nothing.

The Triangle House

The Triangle House first appeared in a dream during a time we were house searching in Seattle. Door after door was closing on us — we were having our bids overridden by huge commercial investors and after half a year of attempts and heartbreak, we were starting to become bitter about the whole home buying process.

When we first came across the listing, we laughed aloud as I had literally described the structure in my dream to Jonah that morning. We were now thinking creatively and had extended our search to beyond the city... the A-frame cabin was in a mysterious seaside town that neither of us were familiar with. We decided to playfully book a weekend trip just to follow the breadcrumbs.

We fell in love with the house, the stormy port town, the slower pace of life. We made an offer that week. Even without having a job yet in the town, we knew if it were meant to be the support would follow.

Somehow everything fell into place over the months that followed. The owners accepted our offer even with the tiny down payment which is what we could afford at the time. Jonah found a job at the local wood mill. Our new life was calling to us and we were answering the invitation into the mystery.

When we moved into that first home, I was a transforming, postpartum mother. There were times where I was exhausted to the bone - feeling stuck inside my own story. At times I felt like I was pushing a rock up a hill — I knew new motherhood would pose challenges, but I hadn't expected it to feel so isolating. As a mystic and artist, I couldn't relate to the mainstream soccer mom ideal. I had distanced myself from many old friendships; many of my former maiden friends I now felt estranged from with my new title and responsibilities. Those early years of living in the Triangle House were a very inward time of Self inquiry and deep healing. Most of our neighbors in the community were elders and we didn't have any blood relatives nearby. Life was very much, eat, work, sleep (when possible) and enjoy the tender sweet moments or miracles in between.

It felt like it took all our creative capacities to keep the ship afloat. I learned so much during that time about the ways in which culture doesn't truly support young families. Without a village, there really is this pull your bootstraps up attitude for the nuclear household. Culture has normalized the experience of burnt out, overworking parents. I was frustrated and could feel in my cells there was another way.

I didn't know then that part of my soul's journey in this lifetime is to be sent to places in the world that need purification so that I can cleanse and activate the lands and study my surroundings to learn what's needed for the heart of humanity. At the time, I knew we had been divinely called to that small town and it was where we were meant to be, but it didn't make it any easier. The winters were long, cold, and grey and there really was no other choice in the isolation but to face the parts of myself that I'd been avoiding unknowingly for so many years.

It was in that Triangle Temple that I experienced my deepest darkest nights of the soul. I shattered so many illusions of my ego and stripped myself bare of old identities. I faced the darkest aspects of my shadow that had been hiding while distracted in the faster paced life of a young maiden in the city. Because life then often felt challenging, I was invited to look at all the places I still felt victim to my experiences. All the places I gave my power away by feeling beholden to circumstance. It really was my maiden-to-mother rite of passage — but like the rouge version without proper integration support from a beloved community.

I did eventually create some of the most deep, profound, and soulful bonds with a few other mothers in the community — not before I did the work necessary to come into vibrational resonance with them though.

Slowly, throughout the years in this mystical grey seaside town... I started to emerge into this true-er, more whole and capable version of myself. I had my first experiences with Shamanic healing and soul retrieval, and soon after I began to remember the work I was destined to facilitate in this lifetime.

After the birth of my son, I began my trainings with different healing modalities and started to blossom into offering my work to the world.

Over the years in the Triangle House, I would hear a whisper saying, "just keep fixing this place up."

We'd spend our weekends painting the walls, going to the salvage yard — landscaping gardens. As the money trickled in, we'd funnel it all back into beautifying the space. Eventually — the fixer upper home transformed into a temple.

I began hosting my private healing sessions and retreats in the space.

On weekends we'd have small parties and celebrations, we'd create projects and were present to the tender ages of our little babies who brought laughter and light even throughout the most trying of times. We really did enjoy being parents and felt blessed in some ways for the isolation that gave us a lot of time to be fully immersed in the experience of it. In some ways it felt like getting a master's degree in conscious parenting because there was no escaping the round the clock duty. No grandparents in town to support, and only a small handful of community that we resonated with. The lack of distraction and support brought us back again and again to home life, being the center of the universe.

Jonah and I really were a team at that time — we were each other's support; emotionally, mentally, financially, spiritually. We got to experience a profound kind of love that comes from knowing each other so intimately in every way.

When we were camping on the land it became clear that in order to fully establish our new life on the Island, it would mean surrendering our old.

We were being asked to commit to the land and the mission that was laid out before us here. It took time and courage, but finally we mustered to put our beloved jewel, our art project of the last decade up on the market. As always, we were following the guidance of the divine – even when fear was present.

When the Triangle House sold — she sold for nearly double what we listed her for. The listing had gone a bit viral and there had been a bidding war — we received letters, homemade videos, and offer-after-offer of eager beings ready to purchase our home.

On the one hand I was floored. She still needed a new roof, her septic system was ancient and though we had spent years remodeling and designing, we did it on our working-class budget and her interior was still pretty shabby chic...

On the other hand — it made perfect sense. That quiet unwavering voice that guided us to keep pouring our love into the space year after year. People were responding to the frequency that had been cultivated and God was rewarding a divine assignment fully honored and completed.

If we Pray

If we pray to be peaceful — we aren't necessarily air lifted to a quiet sunny grassy meadow, but rather shown all ways we have been at war with ourselves.

If we pray for riches — we may be invited to look at all our limiting programming and self-sabotage patterning first.

If we pray for healthy, whole relationships, we may be handed some strong lessons first in the way of unhealthy dynamics so we can truly understand the polarity and appreciate the safe sanctuary of a positive and nourishing relationship when it arrives.

We humans are dynamic creatures. I feel we don't give ourselves nearly enough credit for learning to operate these intricate technologies of the body / mind / spirit. For existing in a world that in many ways has been designed to keep us operating on low level survival mode — to see beyond illusions and remember our original essence and what we're truly capable of feeling is a huge feat.

The path of self-mastery does not reward and anoint us without first cultivating and refining us. This path invites us into deep into Self inquiry, at all times. It reminds us that yes, we are both the map and key, though work is needed to unlock the mystery and awaken from the slumber.

On this path we learn that it was never about all we could accomplish — it's not the outer accolades or imaginary finish line. It's the cultivation of our consciousness. It's who we are being, how we are, what we feel along the way.

From the Village to the Temple

We continued our home search while camping. Without real internet connection – I was prompted to take a break from my private practice and tune into the lands, write, be fully present with the children.

The East side of the Island, which previously felt like a no – started to beckon us to keep an open mind. Since once again, the doors weren't opening where we thought we wanted to be, we expanded our horizon to hear where we were being called.

When a fixer upper home appeared in a jungle road near the ocean, we went to tour it. There were many charming features, including a triangle window in the main bedroom, which felt like a little wink from our beloved triangle house. The entire neighborhood was off grid, and we were walking distance to a private swimming cove.

The signs were there, and we said yes.

At the same time – a small site appeared on the market on the South of the Island. This little jewel on "Pele" street – was showing herself to also have a mission with us.

The homes closed on the same day, and it felt like giving birth to twins. We went from camping being fully humbled to the Earth with no running water, to having two beautiful sites to steward.

It was clear that these weren't ordinary sites, there would be no pushing of our own agendas – but rather once again, listening to the divine guidance for what wanted to be co-created with the lands.

When we arrived to the Jungle site – we soon discovered there was already a Village lifestyle in place. Hidden in these off-grid land sites were other homesteading families sharing similar values. My children could now run between jungle trails to visit friends and share afternoons with aunties. It was like the vision I had been seeding on the larger land site came into form once we let go of the how and surrendered fully into the mystery.

The land site on Pele Street began to get cultivated as a Temple and training grounds for the mystical teachings. The site showed herself as a space for the Goddess. Priestesses from around the Island began to gather and come to know the space as one for them to replenish and commune.

We would take trips together often to set prayers, channel, celebrate, and nourish one another. I would hear this quiet hum that the space erected to support the restoration of organic templates for sisterhood and the mystical arts.

Earth was working through us with this Village home site and the Temple. I began to facilitate trainings reminding women of how life could be; with the domestic life being fully supported by an ecosystem of village community, and the temple life being cocreated with soul family and pristine trainings in honor of the Goddess.

In many ways, the pieces coming together were even dreamier than I could have imagined. So much beauty had been waiting to birth on the other side of the unknown void. If someone could have told me on those wet camping days what we were cultivating, I probably would have allowed myself to relax deeper into trust of the unknown. Deeper into my trust to surrender and allow God to do the heavy lifting.

It really is deep in our surrender to the mystery that the miracles are born.

"God's plan"

Half a year passed as we settled into our new life on the land sites.

One day, I went to a naturopath to explore healthcare support for the family. My menstrual cycles felt more dramatic and painful recently which was not typical for me. Since the symptoms happened to be alive that day – I brought it up casually to the Doctor.

I was surprised when he without hesitation probed deeper into the energetic reason behind the symptoms. He looked at me with this penetrating and confident stare that communicated to me that deep down I already knew the answer.

Tears came rolling down as I reluctantly admitted my deepest secret - which is that I felt in my heart that I was meant to birth another child, but I did not feel it was with my husband.

What?

Why was my body saying this and how did he get this out of me so quickly?

Was this the beginning of the end of my marriage?

Something had felt off for a while now in my relationship. I had oscillated between feeling fully committed and all in and swaying towards the "what if's...." Even though there was so much love and reverence. Something was missing and I couldn't put my finger on it because I hadn't tasted it yet.

Towards the end, the Doc mentioned plant medicines and if I had any experiences there - I told him about my experience with Ayahuasca how I recognized a soul sitting at my feet as a person I've traveled with in many lifetimes. It came out before I could edit. The emotion was there again - I told him about the confusion and heartbreak of not feeling the completion and how that's impacting my desire to procreate another child with my husband.

Why was I telling him all of this? How was any of this relevant?

I came here for acupuncture and restorative self-care and now I was spilling my most internal secrets after twenty minutes? What did this have to do with my symptoms? I wanted to run away.

But as I sat there, time seemed to stop. In my heart, I knew that if the man with the angelic face were to contact me - I would drop what I was doing and be there for the conversation. To explore what was unfinished in lifetimes before. I knew that and I hated admitting it even to myself but especially to this unrelenting stranger because it sounded so ludicrous. There had been little to no confirmation of his recognition of me. Why - a year later was my heart still yearning for the mysterious alchemy that I felt was left unfinished?

And he had his Soulmate and I had mine. He had his Queen, his life partner. He expressed his love and devotion so publicly that evening in ceremony while I sat there and quietly cried.

The doctor put together an herbal recommendation list and asked me what I intended to do with the emotional information I unearthed. I told him it sounded like a conversation with my womb was in order - to really admit to myself my desires and get clear on what I wanted. It always felt so simple to see the blind spots playing out unconsciously in other people, but apparently there was a big well of emotion coming from the suppression of a very inconvenient truth that my body was trying to bury. Of all things, this is not what I wanted to see.

I left the office, feeling raw and exposed. This wasn't the experience of self-care I was envisioning.

I wanted to drive home, crawl under a rock, throw up, scream, just go to sleep. But I had to pee and was also hungry, so I turned my car around and stopped by a local cafe.

I opened the door - and there he was. His back was turned away from the door as he sat with his beloved family.

I ran.

I went back to my car, cried my heart out and drove all the way home.

On the way back, a car was speeding behind me and cut me off sharply. On the back of the car painted across the windshield were the words - "God's Plan."

Intuition

I don't believe we're ever really confused in life so much as we play a little game with ourselves about not knowing.

We forget the full divine plan so that we can experience the magic of remembering it.

Soul always knows the way deep down — to the path of love, career, location.

Soul remembers the map she created and leaves little breadcrumbs and clues for the human to follow.

Being highly sensitive and intuitive adds another element to this game because we have the expanded awareness and prophetic vision to see into timelines that aren't made fully manifest yet. It's almost like we miss the experiences that aren't here yet. I remember missing my children for almost a decade before they finally arrived into my arms.

Our intuition can be the most beautiful gift when we cultivate this ability instead of allowing it to cause frustration between where we are and where we're headed. When we learn to embrace the duality of seeing, knowing, feeling, and desiring future realities while staying firmly planted and grateful for the richness of the now.

This is the dance with reality we get to master — being fully present with what is — while tending to visions for what's to come. Being rooted where we are while staying in devotion to the magic and possibility in the multi-dimensional worlds of the unseen.

Recognition

Over the months the man with the angelic face continued to visit. Often in dreams, or I'd suddenly feel his presence in my energy field.

More memories had now surfaced, other lifetimes and other roles. Leadership together in other dimensions. A vision of a huge dragon spirit that showed herself to be our original soul essence that was split into two parts to come fulfill a mission on Earth.

As much as I tried to get this man out of my consciousness, his memory remained, and in his distance, he continued to teach me things about my own soul.

Eventually I felt exhausted by the persistence and began to set boundaries. Something I'd learned in my years training as a psychic medium is that we always have sovereign control and can tell the spirit beings of other planes what we're available for or not.

I did womb clearings, heart clearings, energy recalls, rituals to close out any old karma. With him – nothing seemed to work.

Once while driving he came to me again with another devotional message telling me to "trust" - he told me to keep some hope alive, even if it was only an ember. He let me know that he remembered what I had done for our people in Atlantis. I burst into tears.

What was this message and why did it get such an emotional response from me?

I'd heard years before in a reading that I had a big impact in Atlantis and that I'd be drawing from that lifetime for leadership in this one, but until now the memories hadn't resurfaced for me.

I was tired of being shaken up in this way and I decided to let him know.

"ENOUGH!"

I screamed. I'd had enough.

I was standing in the kitchen and felt like I had reached a peak. It had been years now of signs, synchronicities and little reminders that kept this man alive in my consciousness even when I tried to forget him.

Before I could think of what I was doing I began to speak aloud to him; assertively.

"If this is really you... if I'm not making this up, show yourself in the physical. Show yourself. I'm starting to question if I'm losing it. You come to me in my dreams, you're there telepathically vividly speaking your adoration and support, but never have you ever offered me the validation in this physical realm. How can I continue to trust this? If this is really you speaking to me, I need you to show up and recognize me now. In this seen world, HERE."

I was crying and shaking. The fire of my feminine rage pulsing through me, unrepressed. I was tired of the connection to this man and how much confusion it brought me — if it was all just a delusional fantasy, I needed to break the spell. I was married, to a man I loved very much. Why was this still happening? Was I cursed?

Once again, I cried until I had no more tears left to cry.

The following afternoon I went to pick up my children from school. I arrived early and decided to meditate in my car.

I closed my eyes and sank into a deep calm state. For a moment, letting go of the world around me, fully surrendering my thoughts and floating above the Earth plane.

Something snapped me back into my body a few

moments later... I opened my eyes suddenly and looked up. There he was. The man with the angelic face was here - at my kid's school.

He was a few feet away from me and I saw the back of his head, slowly walking towards the children. I felt nerves move up my entire body as I sat there mustering the courage to walk towards him and go pick up my son. I felt sick — but somehow rooted in knowing I needed to go confront this mysterious dragon man who had been such a huge part of my journey in the non-physical realms.

I walked over to the main gate where the children were and said "Hello."

He turned around casually at first, then did a swift double take when he saw that it was me. His eyes met mine and for a brief second, his entire body spoke the language of recognition. I felt his energy burst from his skin, like his soul took a leap forward to come meet mine.

For a moment, time stood still.

I noticed how tired he looked. Handsome as ever, but so tired in his soul.

What was he doing here? It turned out his daughter had just enrolled in my son's class.

"I thought you lived on the other side of the Island?"
He asked me.

I fumbled over my words. A part of me wanting to
leap into his arms and hold him close and ask him
everything about his life and his perspectives and
where he's been and how he felt. The other part of
me wanting to run the other direction as fast as I
could.

The other part apparently held more gravity because
after a few words of politely answering his questions —
I turned around and walked away. It was all I could do
to stay in my body, two minutes had felt like eternity,
and I was still digesting the shock of him being there
after our telepathic conversations that I was beginning
to question the validity of.

It felt like confirmation. All this time, it really was him
speaking to me... I wasn't fabricating some illusion.
I had known this deep down in my heart, though
somehow this moment of connection felt like what
my soul had needed to trust herself more.

I drove home in shock. If our soul connection was
this deep — why didn't he verbally communicate his
recognition of me? Was he repressed or in denial?
or maybe afraid of crossing a boundary in his own
relationship?

All these questions I had for him surfaced and I realized how much my heart was still longing to be close to him.

That evening when I was processing, I heard the familiar voice of my soul whisper to me "You cannot keep running away from this. You need to show yourself."

It was though a force much greater than me took over when I wrote to him that evening with a message letting him know how synchronicity brought us to this side of the Island. I told him about the Village, the Temple being built and the way in which we were listening to Source to guide the process every step of the way.

I didn't know why I was telling him but that palpable force to speak was there again, so I heeded the call. Three weeks went by before there was any response. I had just awoken from a dream where he and I had come to meet in this empty classroom in the etheric realm. I arrived as he was sitting there waiting for me — our joining together came at long last, and we were eager to see each other. I ran over to him, and we embraced. We were equally excited to share what we had been learning during our life studies away from each other, and to listen in to each other's mastery.

I was slowly waking up and processing the dream

when his message response came through. Brief —
apologizing for the delay and giving thanks for the
continuous life update.

I could sense underneath the brevity, the weight of
words left unsaid and questions unanswered. He
didn't have to tell me for me to know that it took him
some time to craft an appropriate response. One that
was kind and sincere yet contained. It felt to me that
he had curiosity and desire to lean in and remember
more but restrictions or societal pressures to withhold
deeper intimacy because of the marital agreements he
had in place.

"What a weird world we set up with little invisible
cages for our soul" I thought to myself.

I responded to him without hesitation, again that
cosmic force taking over me.

"Thank you. There's no rush or expectation on this
end ever. I can feel all the stewards of the sacred
weaving in a cosmic council whether in conversation
or not."

I meant it. For whatever reason all I ever really wanted
to convey to this man was, "I love you unconditionally.
No matter the lifetime; you will always be free
with me."

Trusting the Heart

Once in one of my group coaching containers — a woman was reviewing her life and asked what she felt the difference between settling and accepting was. One of the participants chimed in that she felt settling meant forgoing your core values. While I agreed, I added that settling can also mean sharing a baseline of core values with someone / something, but overriding the symptoms in your body or the longing in your heart that's guiding you elsewhere.

As women, it's common to tell ourselves "Oh this is fine. I should just be happy, look at all these blessings!" While yes, having a solid gratitude practice is a key to our thriving — not at the expense of overriding that inner voice of truth. Remaining so loyal that we betray ourselves will corrode our wellbeing in the long term.

It takes devotion to be able to listen in to hear where we're being guided... we can simultaneously enjoy the beauty that life is offering while understanding and accepting when our fate is calling us toward a different destiny.

We can fully love and appreciate what's in front of us, while listening and honoring when we're being beckoned somewhere else.

It's hard to follow a call before physical evidence appears. Maybe the hardest thing in the world. We're so heavily conditioned to look for proof, to trust the seen physical reality as law. When so much of the magic of existence dwells far beyond our mind's comprehension.

Before we learn to cultivate this trust of our intuition, we'll be living a life written for us. When we lean in, clear our minds, bodies and spirits of the distortion impressed upon us by confused society — it becomes a lot easier to trust navigating life beyond logic.

As we continue to follow the breadcrumbs, take leaps of faith, and trust this divine intelligence that is way vaster than us — we begin to build trust with this secret and holy part of ourselves. We learn to quiet the outer voices and the projections from the conditioning of others, and we cultivate this un-shakable knowing that we are right about things without even having to know how we know. We may find we don't need to consult the authorities as often or look to the external for proof of what we've always known deep inside. We just know in our hearts and that's enough.

Heart knows. She's stubborn too. We can play pretend all we want. Suppress, avoid, distract – but her truth remains. No matter how much we try to bury it for convenience's sake, the heart will always hold the knowing. If we dare to look, we will find within her all the truths we seek; she holds the entire map and key to the cosmos and our specific role within this divine orchestration called life.

Truth

What a radical act to choose truth in a world that seems to fear it over everything.

We've been taught to behave, to wear masks, to keep the realest and rawest parts of our being hidden away, tamed, or repressed.

For most people, in most environments — truth doesn't feel safe to express.

Truth isn't always convenient. Sometimes truth means setting fire to the illusions we've created in our lives. Sometimes it means losing people who can't handle the purest parts of our soul. Truth isn't always pretty or palatable. But it's the only thing that sets us free.

Dream Journal

"Today I cried with the rains – I mourned the truth that I can no longer suppress: that my union in its current form with Jonah is over. We saw a vision together last night: together in a castle – surrounded by guards – protectors. We were talking at a candle lit table, holding unconditional love for each other to have our own processes, just witnessing.

For now, it was time for me to leave. I had to follow the scent of a flower that was calling me. It was no longer optional to stay, my soul knew it was time to go. I hopped on a horse and followed the scent; found a trail to a new castle. This one wasn't surrounded by guards – just open, loving, magical, free, naked, dancing people. Pure love frequency. Jonah stayed behind – choosing not to join the party. I felt home there in this new land, whereas he felt foreign and left out.

It was certain though. I had no choice but to answer a new call to my destiny - and allow him the freedom to fully answer his."

Luana

My love, I felt you circling me for so long. My third child. I could feel your spirit before you entered my body: serene and grounded, more equanimous than my other children. When you left, I felt alone in my grief. I wanted to expedite the pain, so I told myself I was done. I felt strong and empowered by choosing to move on and let go.

But grief does not work like that.

She commands to be felt completely - she may hide out for a while, but her story remains in the body until we honor her fully. One day years later, the sadness of you visited me again and I was taken by surprise. I didn't know I still had to forgive myself for not growing, birthing, and raising you.

When I finally let you go — it was by a fire underneath the stars. I held my womb and dropped down to the Earth.

You weren't joining me in this lifetime, and I could not remain in purgatory waiting. I heard you whisper to me "not all babies are meant to come straight to Earth. Some are first meant to set you free."

A shooting star lit up the sky and I knew my grieving you was complete.

Rise

Through the tears, we can always choose to rise. Continue on with the journey - trusting the setbacks as necessary re-routes.

If we came to anchor in great light onto the planet - we will be tested, expanded, humbled, and broken open to evolve into beings who can accomplish the mission. Not necessarily in the way our minds mapped it out but the way our hearts truly need.

Unconditional Love

During the years of feeling the presence of the man with the angelic face, I felt like I was living between worlds. Here I was, married to a kind, devoted, brilliant man — the most loving father. I was trying so hard to be content with this reality reflection. To fully accept the union and be grateful for the blessings all around me... and yet my heart continued to long for this mysterious stranger. A man who seemed to be denying our connection — or perhaps was afraid of what that would mean for his own life if he did fully face it.

Sometimes the energy would feel peaceful and steady — I would completely surrender my feelings to the divine and let it all go. At other times it would feel like a force overtaking my entire being. It would wake me up in the night in a sweat. Like I knew that I would walk one thousand miles to get to this man, to honor this energetic pull, look into his eyes and uncover this mystery.

It'd been over two years now of me oscillating between wondering if he was my genetic equal, my twin soul and future lover, or if he was a fallen angel placing a curse on my life.

Wasn't love supposed to feel good?

How could a force like this continue to be present after everything I was doing to close it up?

So many times, I'd tried to close the door on this and yet again, the feelings would resurface.

Some nights I could feel his energy near me, his gentle breath on my neck. I would think about all the things I would talk to him about if we were in person. All the ways in which his council was the missing piece in my life. I felt in my heart no one else would understand things in a way that he would be able to.

If this man was truly the other half of my soul and we had a mission to play out — wouldn't he remember that too?

Why would he continue to repress this?

———————————————————

Because it was never actually about him.

Of course, it was, but it wasn't.

He was the muse. The mirror. He was this book wanting to be written and he wasn't going away until it was. He was the representation of devotional love that was missing in how I was showing up in my real union. He may have been my mirror soul, because he was a stark reflection of ME and all the parts of me that still needed to be felt and transmuted into unconditional love...It was never about him, rather what he represented.

His lack of validation and physical presence was one of the greatest gifts I could have received on my journey, because it sent me back to myself over and over again. Each time, bringing me closer and closer into union with Source.

It was never about him; it was always about returning fully to the true beloved — within.

The key purpose of any powerful relationship beyond a physical union is purification and inner cultivation. Every time we make it about the other person, we are sent back to ourselves. That's where the true healing, awakening, and ascending in consciousness takes place if we allow it. The most radical awakenings can happen through separation, whether that's through death of a loved one, ending of a relationship or not having things pan out the exact way our ego desired.

True unconditional love loves us so deeply it will show us all the ways in which we're still not free.

It's a kind of love that won't reward you when you're codependent, needy or controlling. It won't reward you if you are stuck in your illusions or operating from fear.

This kind of love loves you so deeply it wants you to face all the aspects of yourself that you've avoided — the things you would never be able to see without the steady hum of this kind of love staying present in the background of your life.

This kind of love won't let you go. It loves you so deeply that no matter how many times you beg, scream, curse to be released from the agreement, it remains.

This kind of love isn't about another person, so much as it's about union with God. Union with your own soul.

Until you truly face yourself and listen to what your soul is guiding you to do, you will continue to loop and recycle the experience of the illusion of separation. You simply cannot come into physical sacred union with this kind of love if you're not in union with the most high.

This is an ultimate love — it is not about hooking into another person.

This kind of love is here to bring you home to inner union, and the true beloved within.

Dancing with the Mystery

We don't have to know how it will all turn out to follow the next step and then the next.

Nothing in life unfolds exactly as we envision it - that's one of the most beautiful things about dancing with the mystery.

When we're surrendered to what spirit wants to flow through us instead of being fixated on chasing what everyone else is doing, we're able to fully enjoy the only thing that's real - this present moment.

Trust your divine plan.

Take time to quiet the noise. Listen to those whispers that are always, always there.

Choose the belief that everything is always working out for the highest good. That way, when challenges arise (as they will again and again) you know it's another phase of time supporting you to cultivate resilience and fine tune your adaptability. Humbling you and reminding you the truth of what really matters most.

Being in the flow of life as the witness rather than trying to force or control is key.

The divine plan will guarantee to surprise us both with events more miraculous and ones more grief filled than we ever could have imagined.

Being willing to wholeheartedly experience all of it without repression is the gold. Keeping an open heart rather than becoming jaded.

We are conduits for the divine, only here in these bodies for a brief period of time, so why not dance the most beautiful courageous dance while we're here?

"Life is not a problem to be solved.
It is a mystery to be lived"
-Unknown

About the Author

Saige Esmaili is an Iranian-American visionary, mother, spiritual mentor, and designer of sacred spaces. Her work is both other worldly mystical while down-to-earth accessible. While as a psychic she walks between many realms, she also embraces a refined reality in the modern world that women of all kinds find relatable. From designing temples to facilitating transformational alchemy, all her work exists to open doors to magical realities.

Acknowledgments

Thank you to God, spirit, source, unconditional love — the life force spirit pulsing through all things; the true beloved. I AM because of God and for that I am grateful.

Thank you to my mother, Jill. To the one who's womb brought me physically to this plane of existence. My mentor, my friend and my spiritual ally. Thank you for always seeing me, endlessly supporting my wild ideas and for teaching me the meaning of unconditional love through your devotion to your children and your own evolution.

Thank you to the Goddess that is this Earth. My sister, my mother, my anchor, my love. Everything I create here is in honor of your beauty.

To my mentors, seen and unseen. The ones I've met and received face to face nectar and teachings from, to the ones who've impacted me through their energy and teachings. Kumu Leina'ala - thank you for the ancient mystery teachings and Hawai'ian wisdom you steward with so much power and passion. Thank you for remembering who I was so I could better remember myself in your reflection. Lalah Delia, Alyson Charles, Clarissa Pinkola Estes, and so many more guides on the path. My soul wife and creative midwife Paola Ucelo. My Atlantean sister Sam. My right hand fairy and assistant Shyann.

To Christine Gutierrez, thank you Earth angel, for feeling the pulse of this book wanting to birth even when I did not. Thank you for reminding me there was a message wanting to come through and that books have a soul of their own.

To my clients. To every woman who's allowed me the deepest of honor of being in service to the sanctuary of her sacred inner world. It's in your reflection and authentic sharing that I've learned most about the heart of the feminine and what we need to truly thrive. This work is not something I take for granted and I appreciate every breath, every tear and every truth you have ever shared with me. Thank you.

Thank you to my children, Tula and Lux. My real gurus and teachers who daily expand my consciousness and challenge me to become a more evolved woman. Thank you for initiating me into my favorite role of all: mother.

And to you Jonah. My best friend and husband of almost a decade - the most loving and devoted papa to our babies. Thank you, for loving me and being such a powerful support. For the hours of shamanic journeying, adventuring, connecting, crying, visioning, birthing and building we've done. Thank you for loving and seeing me in a way that no one else ever has. Thank you for embodying the divine masculine. Thank you for believing in me, and walking alongside me as this book took us on a ride and initiated us into an even deeper kind of intimacy. I love you.

Printed in the United States
by Baker & Taylor Publisher Services